BOOKS BY STAN RICE

FEAR ITSELF

FEAR ITSELF

Poems by
STAN RICE

ALFRED A. KNOPF
New York 1995

THIS IS A BORZOI BOOK
PUBLISHED BY ALFRED A. KNOPF, INC.

Library of Congress Cataloging-in-Publication Data

Rice, Stan
    Fear itself : poems / by Stan Rice.—1st ed.
      p. cm.
    ISBN 0-679-44441-6
    I. Title.
  PS3568.1295F43 1995   95-42770
  811'.54—dc20   CIP

Manufactured in the United States of America
First Edition

FOR ANNE AGAIN

Fear not lest ye be feared.

§ CONTENTS

CONTENTS

FEAR ITSELF

You might call it
A wasted sea-change
My trip to Haiti
In '78.
I was constantly afraid.
I was the only white man
I'd see for days
And I didnt like it.
I had done nothing wrong
But felt constantly guilty.
Not that Haiti
Was an easy experience.
The police were murderers.
The cab drivers were thieves.
Everywhere were posters
Of the Dictator's face
Under the phrase
President For Life.
You had to get written permission
From the Government
To go from one town to another.
Teenaged boys wanting to be
My "guide" would hassle me until
I'd go back to my hotel
To hide and drink. Hiring one
Kept the other ones off you.
Having lived so long
Under tyranny
The citizens of Port-au-Prince
Wore expressionless masks.
But even given all this
I was about as relaxed
As a pistol. I felt
Undefended, morally naked,
Paranoid. I had a hair-trigger
Temper. Only in one sense
Was the sea-change not wasted:
I was the nigger.

For the tenth day in a row
I eat roast chicken and horseradish.
I eat it in a booth by the bar
Where the young women in office dresses
Lean near one another talking in hushed
Lyrical voices about the office. To women
Men are taller, hairier versions of themselves
But to men women are inexplicable
And I'll probably eat roast chicken tomorrow.

§ *THE REPORT*

I have gone in
To bear witness
And report back:
Chaos, sir.
Homicidal madmen
Control all.
No order, no plan,
No objective
But murder itself.
Even ants
Do not do this
To one another.
Some are red.
Some are black.
There is an objective:
To route the Other.
Truckloads
Of drunken men
When finished killing
Passersby
Kill each other.
I see no hope
But for this carnage
To run its course.
Bloodlust and sadism
And vengeance
Are rampant.
There is nothing to report.
Can this be human?
I can only say
I have never witnessed
Such pleasure.

§ A BOY'S SATAN

1.

I will tell you
Where the Devil lived.
He lived in
The padlocked
Iron-wire toolshed
Where everything
Was the color of rust
Which is the color the Devil is.
I was told to Stay Out Of There,
Because it contained
Black widows, scorpions, and wasps.
Though this was true the real
Reason I was not allowed
Inside the shed was because
That's where the Devil hung his head
To rest it while the pure evil
Of the Daylight Moon did his duties.

2.

At the end of the gravel alley
In the darkness was where
The Devil In Overalls
Kept chickens. Once one of his roosters
Escaped down the narrow space between
Our garage and his fence, with no way out.
And the Devil offered me fifty cents
(A fortune!) to go in and bring out the rooster
Because, you see, 'he couldnt fit.'
I said I certainly would and went in
And when I got a few feet from the rooster
It went insane and as uncatchable
As a ball of flaming razorblades
And I backed out instantly to see
The Devil in his Overalls grinning at me,
Saying, "Well, son, youll never get rich like that,"
And I said, right out loud,

"Not the Devil himself
Could get that rooster," and the Devil's eyes
Rolled up slightly so I could see
The whites below and his Overalls
Filled up more with himself
And he said, in an oily drawl,
"It'll come out or starve,"
And I knew that even
Though he had toyed with my life
The Devil was right.

1.

Chocolate cake with 30
Candles fluttering enters.
She carrying it has leaping
Cheekbones and lips.
This is when life eats death
Like a grape popsicle.
Two naked legs are left,
And the purple muzzle
Of that particular god.

2.

Something got me,
But passed quickly.
I left my afterimage
On the alley fence.
Who can be quick
Enough to dodge
Dread? Even atoms
Admit their cowardice.
And quarks go solemnly
Inward to contemplate
Their parents' deaths.
It takes skill, but
The darkness can be
Slipped. You can
Walk down the long
Black alley without
Whistling; ungot;
Imitating the molecules
In your own head.

3.

For fear that
I will see myself
I lower the blinds
At night so no black
Glaze will reflect me.
And turn the television
On so I'll be invisible
In it. Now it is time to face
The god in the mental.
Orifices ordinary
As laundry rooms fill
With deities.
Getting up off the couch
Feels like the third
World War. I attempt to
Adjust my glasses
200 times. Still
My ears hurt.
This is the effect
Of nightfall on some.
In the shining
Mercury of the TV
Goat's afterbirth
I fear I'll see
Myself.

4.

Ah, April. Sarcasm
Eludes me. I'm truly
In admiration of being
Human. Who can gather
And adequately praise
The details? The newly
Leafed crape myrtle
Softly shivers. Almost
Instantly the frost-burnt

Banana leaves unfurl
New leaves from
Their stumps. The roses
Gradually outswell
Their virginity;
Bulge purple through
Splitting calyxes.
My mirrored gazing-globe
On its black pedestal
On the deck outside my
Studio thirty feet up
Shows me as a forked
Red dot. April,
Ah, when the details
Come back.

5.

The greenery, the dustmotes
In the sunbeams, the gods,
Are in alliance.
So that I will be
Blinded by variety
I bend to their needles.
This won't hurt a bit.

I know my enemy's beauty,
Fear's beauty.
Being fondled
By its bone glove.
It blows on my fur,
And the black hairs' silver roots
Twice shine.
Once with fear, once with love.

God made in His image
The lowland gorilla,
In whose apt black glory
He sits, eating the greenery
Of paradise. Algae,
Having mastered the Art,
Created a brain
That saw itself, knew itself,
Jerked itself off
In the milky woods,
Lay in pine needles
Remembering pine needles.
Therefore pity the Lord,
Who cannot fathom
These smoothskinned offspring
Who laugh at their father
And His ape heart.

§ NEW YORK TWILIGHT FROM 63rd FLOOR

White moon centered in window, far away,
But near my senses.
Citicorp Building reflecting sunset
Same steel white.
Suddenly, staring at nothing, I see it.
All is gradual.
All.
The Himalayas are gradual.
The long love that ripens, whitens.
For a moment, a moment, I am immortal.
Death looks right through me!
Between Central Park and the Empire State Building,
Innumerable purples.
Moon reaches the pulled-up venetian blinds.
Time must have passed.
Every detail of the twilight scene
Is transfixed in its fictional state
Like airbubbles in ice. Let this last,
Lord. Let me
Take from it
A lesson, a method.
The senses are our messengers, our angel.
Why so rarely?
Little crystal helicopters
Crisscross the violet cartoon.
Thank you, thank you!
What did I see?
The focused, frozen tableau of the gradual.
My awe. Its clarity. One.
Night comes on.
Moon 'goes.'
Citicorp Building whitened by floodlights.
If only I could never be the same.

Clear eyed, hair silver, animal.
Wanting, still, only
The red virgin. To rend
In the name of Love.
Placing himself in extremis
Because extremis is mythic.
Then lamenting the hardship.
Of marble. Of love lost. Of Crete.
I look back at him in a
Black and white photo and it's as if
He were always
A black and white photo.
Always looking for the
Red flesh of the virgin
To twist him like
Cellophane in flame.

§ DEADLETTERS

What more happy song than one's lot?   LOUIS ZUKOFSKY

DEADLETTER 1

That marble statue
Is the color
Of a glass of milk
On which the shadow
Of the head of the drinker
Has fallen.

DEADLETTER 2

Eliminate fear that experience is dangerous.
Lock stork in dark.
Undergo Woolworths.
Vomit the skeleton and feel lighter, wiser.
The candleflame leans toward the crack in the door.
The lure of the flesh is felt even by Linguists.
Words fling down their skins
On the lockerroom floors.
Piano peels lid to its harp.
Each tension, tenderness, offered.
Glue decal to mirror
And see the truth twice.
May the cribs be re-filled.
But with what?

DEADLETTER 3

Rake rose garden, rake grave.
He tied his horse to his rowboat
So that neither could stray; by the Nile.
It is said of the seventh wave, it is said.
The marshlily, the cradle of beetles, spines on its belly;
The kingfisher, the tern, the sea eagle.
I am thinking my father was browner,
And my daughter a wave carved in marble.
I am dressed for the dream
And she's in the tub, and in the mirror.
To choose is possibly to love the wrong bather.
If anger continuously follows on anger
What scale to weigh them, to end it?
The song loathes its limits.
The raked grave appears loved.
The illusion is tender,
Intended.

DEADLETTER 4

Blow over, anger.
Blow through the painting, the grass cottage.
Cows have been milked, sleep.
Sheep in a mass come to the watertank.
The deer who fear them flee them, so many.
Down slope to sea the sunset, peach and silver,
Slides. Lucid. Liar.
Blow over, anger.
Blow through me, hay-needles.
I walk back to the fire.

DEADLETTER 5

Be tender, subtle
To the mammals
With backbones
That branch.
There will come grief,
And an end to yearning, a turning
To liquid of muscle.
Be subtle, tender
To your double.

DEADLETTER 6

It is not an art at all,
Watching the shadow of the building
Fall on the roses. Not an art to note
Color crumble from wall
Scarlet in inches to orange.
Crickets chirk in the dark.
They, also, are not art.
I have tasted the sweetness of the mental sugar
And ruined it by coughing thereon.
Clogged the colander of stars. Yuk.
Soon the whole courtyard will be in shadow
Like the roses, as before,
And I will go home to more
Of these irrational songs.

DEADLETTER 7

I did not want
A perfect pig,
Starry-eyed,
Pink as rose,
But that is what
I got. God knows
I tried to give it back.
All I wanted was a normal dog.
But got a Sorrow, Power,
Archangel-Hog
So nearly perfect
I wanted to jerk off
Its head, but it stuck on,
There, in the dark,
A blur of pig,
Rosepink, rose-fed,
And by all measures
But my own stone
Dead.

DEADLETTER 8

You have walked far enough
In the shoes of Beauty
Take them off
Your hose are bloody
For God's sake
Put on the ones in the bag.

DEADLETTER 9

       —lifting my hat
in the grey elevator, very moved
by her white neck, red turtleneck, white neck.

The image lives on in two zones.
       Where the dead have been
Life combs its hair.

       You have to be a hairless bone
       For the gods to drink you
       Through a straw
       From marble.

       —my throbbing hat, lifted.

Under her silks,
Her image.

DEADLETTER 10

O bicycle of thought, O drooling scythe,
O pinbud, O verbless book,
O bobbin from the cerebellum, O biblical jaw,
O half-cream ocean, thermometer's red liquid,
O messenger ali in brown, O pale day's blackbirds,
To the lake to roost for the night, to rustle,
O eyes floating in kohl, O vodka in Cairo,
O British tree the only purple in Thebes,
O coil of feces just made and still smoking,
O newly born musk ox struggling to stand
In the afterbirth shining like mercury,

Redeem us.

DEADLETTER 11

Moonless midnight,
Same black as lake. The morning glories
Fuck-me-purple.
The humans lean on their elbows in windows.
The motor oil twists from its hole.
Taken as charms or riddles we have stand-up hair,
Can witness, amazed.
And the beanpod fattens until each bean is a bump.
There is another kind of purpose as well:
Blossom as urge,
Birth as Beyond The Will. The mint creeps
Downhill. The comatose woman's womb still contracts.
Rim gleams where the lake touches dirt.
The humans lean on their elbows in windows.
Full of purpose, good intentions.
All their purposes forgiven.

DEADLETTER 12

While sane, expose,
Like the orange and silver
Fish on ice.
Show
The jellied eye. So,
When the un-sane comes,
You will be sold,
And, in the fishfry, not
Alone.

DEADLETTER 13

In the dignity of grief's
Measure feet
Drag the dust.

Go, rhythms, have a life.

Burden the deadletter carrier.

We trust your riddles. You
Are our pieces, gathered, errors
Patterned.

DEADLETTER 14

Let the few words
Written stand for all the spoken
Ones. We have memories
But not the art of it.
As we lie down in different beds
It is clear we are each other's
Issue. Here, stranger,
These are for you.

§ *BY AIDS*

Sweet place
Where mind comes
To nurse the absurd
Let in my
Last words.
They are, "John. John."

One who is tall and flesh becomes
The white rabbit Death, in Maine,
In the aluminum walker,
Who once was tall and bald in black leather.

We do not know
What crisp lake must be crossed on foot
To reach the cave of black-leathered rabbits.

Crossing the room
In the aluminum walker
He opens the refrigerator.
A white gasp!

25 half-gallon jugs of sensual experience,
Each labeled, "John's. John's."

The goons are at the gate again.
Beware my friends,
Lest they be you.
We are in the skeletal stage.
The bloom is still in the wood.
Beware my friends
Self-censorship
For the book unwritten
Is the book burned.
Literalists of all stripes
Wipe their knives
On their long skirts
And take back the night.
The devil is always naked.
His pants are always too tight.
He can rape you with a beam of light.
Beware my friends.
They beat the gate
To the same old tune,
For they have seen Satan,
And they mean well,
And they are the goons.

Water plunges always downward.
Chocolate cake ablaze with candles.
This is more proof than Dread can handle
That what matters is what we make.
The bottle of liquid-paper is choked up.
The statue perpetually removes its sandle.
Up! rise the bugeyed goldfish to eat.
Tubeworms twenty feet long
Live in boiling undersea heatvents.
No head, no tail, no gut, just worm.
Completely independent of the sun.
We have darkened the room for the birthday cake.
Each flame thinks its personal struggle is: The Fall.
The oilpaint in the tube isnt the same
As the oilpaint of the oilpaint rose

—poem fatally interrupted by phone call.

Sunk below us, all New York.
The treasure in twilight.
Paradise on earth a bath.
Religion and the religious life.
You cannot be all places at once.
That is the talk of a fool.
In the milkchocolate face, green eyes.
Under glass, the slaughter of silk ties.

I thought she said,
"The moonlight of fashion
Will have a dwarf
For dinner there."
We laughed and headed up 56th.
Being in New York
I thought of Mississippi
And described it to her.
A saturated couch is on the porch,
Its human hollows shadowed.
A pitbull named Blossom
Is chained to a stake.
You will pass this place and think
No humans eat dumplings
And redgravy with chicken
Fallen from greysmooth bones.
You will fear to touch the vaginal couch.

In milky sunlight the skyscrapers
Are steel & glass honeycombs.
Central Park is in its sexual fur.
The icerink is not bright.
The religious life is not assuming.
Each distance is an etching and
Each close-up an excretion of emeralds
From psychological holes.

The man by the plateglass
That reflects his red nose and shirt
Is laughing at nothing.
Does inappropriate laughing hurt?
The beggar, also, works.
Though some sit slumped like Rodins.
There is no sleet in August.
The man with the clothes welded to him
Who sits in winter on the Dance Theatre steamvent
Is vacationing in the subway's
Coolness.

I cannot resist the race,
Or the smooth selves.
Each time a car runs over the loose manhole cover
The cover sounds startled.
Soon the steel will be smoother.
Each leaf fluttering against the brick it climbs
Accentuates the essential hunger.
Ten feet
Below the steel sidewalk grate, in
The numberless cigarette butts,
In the crud (call it 'soil'),
Asparkle with gumwrapper foil,
Three little trees,
Alive!
The little resurrections.
The glass pigeon's glass eggs.
The saleswomen like nurses of matter.
The believable: visible. The religion.
The moonlight of fashion having the dwarf for dinner.

§ *PARTIAL DATA*

She is dark gold like a slope of Northern California
Down to the gleaming sealions.
We cannot go back later and add the sincerity.
If analogues are not valid we are doomed, cast out.
Is that long yellow thing in the middle painful?

§ THE PREACHER'S TIMING

                              Oh
The way the preacher stops
And mops his forehead
With his white handkerchief
And glances stage left
As though God stood there
Nodding
Is exquisite.
And the crowd's brainmass is engulfed
By an orgy of agreement
That exceeds the sexual
As the preacher slowly
Stuffs his handkerchief
Back in his breast pocket,
Having paused just the requisite
Number of seconds
For the people to burst into semen- and blood-squirting sticks.

§ *THE GIRLS' SCHOOL LAWN*

The schoolgirls
In white socks
Sit crosslegged
On the lawn.
Their suede thighs
Untied.
I do not drive by.

Where is my friend
Whose beauty and masochism
Would have made her a seeress
At Delphi?

Maybe she is in Buffalo
Teaching creative writing.
Maybe she has gone to Athens
To lie on her back

With legs spread,
Mimicking the scarlet poppy,
Awaiting a marble man who
Will be mean to her so that

She may leave him and be driven
Farther into solitude
And prophecy. Maybe she is on
Her hands and knees in Sonoma County

Mimicking the golden poppy
For the same reason: to work on her tone.
I am afraid for my friend
But she and her fate are not in my

Hands. As she enters her 50s
The bloom of her beauty will go and
Marble men will not come to mistreat her
Into submission and song.

What will my friend sing of then?
Of the fate of the lonely, the rejected.
Of beauty abused. Of the scarlet poppy
Crushed by love's boot. Of the sodomized wren.

Tulip tree
Comes purple cream.
Then the self-pleasuring
Green leaves.
Four notes, one dove, solo.
Below
Go the voiceless worms.
No wonder humans
Are frightened
Of death.
Gentle dumb
Dove isnt.
Well, look. The fly unable to get through the pane of glass
Will continue in its hope to penetrate the transparency
Until it becomes a tie-tack.
The skyscrapers at night
Like embers on ice.
This, says Anne, is the secret:
Yaweh was Satan.
Stop writing about the dead!
Bring before our senses
The slender and supple;
They, also,
Are immortal.
Torch-tongued
One, like sparks
Your small hairs
           these
No one can paint.

§ *FEAR*

It was years before I became unafraid to be known.
Fear is brighter than sea foam.
The Japanese have bred a chicken with black bones.

§ *THE JEWISH VIRGIN*

Relaxed as corn tassle
She sits down on the massive couch.
The down pillows
Accept her as effortlessly
As grass blades accept a folding fawn.
Very still she remains, only her huge
Semitic eyes brownly up and down
Acknowledge she is being spoken to,
And she speaks so softly herself
That to hear her you must lean
Almost near enough to be brushed
By her cascade of chocolate brown hair.
By doing as little as one possibly could do
She has completely dominated the living room.
Her passive delicate beauty
Has drawn everyone else toward her
Like doomed lovers in a sonnet sequence.
And it's 1992, for Christ's sake.

The apples burn,
Greenish through red
Gauze. Firm fluid
Like an eyeball
Is the memory
Of them.

§ PHOTOS OF MY FATHER-IN-LAW SANDING

Where I'm not now
Photos sorrow.
In them Howard
Sands the frame,
Sands the frame
Of blue inlay. Twelve years before
His now known death-date,
Finally,
The frame is smooth.

§ GREAT THE LORD'S GOURD

Though I do not believe
Great must have been the gourd
The Lord God used to dip
Shining matter from voluminous void
And endless the arm
And bones of platinum, nevertheless
Deepspace is so glutted with stars
I should not be surprised
That people dreamed up gourd-using Gods
For otherwise when they opened their eyes
To see the milky blackness that mocks their mortality
They would have been squirted out of their mothers at birth
Like watermelon seeds into instantaneous insanity.

Forget the parrots?
Forget the Haitian
Who ate the embers?

Glazed raisinrolls
In filthy bakery—
Did that raisin just run away?

Forget them?
We dont put fat
On salt in a shrine!

Look, the cow
With the violet udder
Has Rembrandt's
Large yellow head!

This must be some
Modernist juxtaposition
Of mint jelly
And those crushed by earthquakes.

Look! the cow has no head.
That is where the painting stops.
Then begins Rembrandt's ride
Into the modern Dutch dark.

That the Tibetan woman has three husbands
Does not mean she is thrice sweetened by snuff,
Stuffed with lamb,
And as sexually satisfied as a vine.
It means she is beaten three times as much.

Forget them?

We who live here accept the rot
And the toil against it as generally equal,
And we stay alive by letting the good times roll
Out of the neck of the once beautiful queen
Who bent over to see if oysters have eyes
And was yanked from her soul by a roach
In a hairnet and a tuxedo.
Pleasure Measures!
Pleasure Measures!
Even the rocks know this
And the rocks are older than water.

Stop me if youve heard this one . . .
There was this
Cherry laurel in which
Each night at approximately 11
A mockingbird would begin
Its endless watery soliloquy
Until I dont know when,
Because when I went to bed, around 2,
It was always still emitting
The most glorious sound of any animal
In the animal kingdom.
Why this bird did this was a mystery to me
Until one night I went out into the yard
And very far off, almost too far to hear,
Was another mockingbird,
Also singing, and I thought, Well, there you are,
It's a matter of self-enlargement.
Once I knew this it didnt make
The singing less spectacular it just
Made it more causal.

§ SHEER FEARS

I.

Dread red thread, erect.
Nakedness urges aside
Edible delicate shreds;
Unless dress rise.

For barren raiment
Tender entry cries.
Nest nears
Plush place, put apart.
Nectar hardens filaments inside.

Breeze pressures fur
As blur of silver hairs
Half black.
Suckled muscles shine, alive.

Each nerve reaches fact
Creamy as flames.
Sighs lie.
Knowledge mothers
Sensual nameless
Fur of fox.

Blur arches regardless
Of color of cur or Lord.

2.

Pearl compels
Will's shell
To crystalize.

Mouths mount
Moments.
Kill by kill
The marbled roundness
Hollows.

Whose silky rock is this
My tendril thrills?
What is this horrible
Willing solid animal
I swallow?

3.

Rub this
Rib with your
Wet dress.
Raw
As rush of salmon
Am I.
Bear claw
Appears above
In crystal crust.
Its jaws foam red
With my white roe.
Rub, rub
This.
Your dress
Is lawlessness.
I spawn and
Rot in it.

4.

Clouds' coral
Coals in black oak leaves—
Drive on.
Focus nears closure,
Crushed,
As black as root of snowy swan—
Drive on.

5.

Can't constantly be pig-pink
And wakeful as paint.
Must sometimes be azure
As saints.
All life can't be Same Pig
And not once faint
In soft grave's red-cheeked slop.
Must sometimes sleep
Like ice on fur
After massacre.

6.

Doves in laurels,
Plump as shadows,
Leave our sorrows
In leaves of laurels.

§ *PAST MASTER*

If I mash my brain against paper
And it leaves an imprint
Bloody and blue as a map
And I find someone from the past
Who has painted this disaster
He is my master.

§ THE CARTOON MICE

Oh, see the cartoon mice,
How they enter themselves twice,
Then squirt from their own
Eyeballs like weenies of ice.

Oh, they are hideous things,
Curvaceous and sleek and insatiable
As maggots in the corpse of a king
Or a queenfull of snowhite lice.

If we could we would slice
Each of them in half.
But they are as plentiful as atoms
And would only laugh

At us and metamorphose
Into some other thing
Maybe twice as horrible,
Maybe this time with wings.

Behold these scavengers:
Like crawling rhinestones
They scour the bones
White.

These cartoon mice are as fully alive
As any perfection of flesh,
And in our wounds they writhe
And fatten themselves on our death.

Dawn comes silver and peach
To the tops of the tallest trees
Then gradually down and down
Till it touches the fallen leaves,

In whose brainlike moisture they thrive.
Oh, see how their eyes are blind,
And their mouths little satchels of knives,
These mice from our minds.

§ *FALLING AGAIN*

Youre right.
We must fall
In love again.

Nectar must
Come from the wood.
Spring

That does not
Depend on
Flesh alone

      from which time
Rips every

      the leaves
Turn crisp
That were wet
When youth.

I fear you
As you crystalize,
Wilder eyed.

As the white wall
Is insane with the blown tree's shadow.

Again
Ancient
Anew
The fallen

Must fall.

§ NOT IN NEW YORK

When I am not in New York
I think of its intimidating beauty.
It is like being inside a brain
When its owner is sleeping.
The black night air is full of burning people.
In olivegreen rags, in tuxedos.
The yellowcabs move like cancercells in a bloodstream.
Behind every glass door is the mystery of safety or danger.
Everyone is going someplace in particular.
When I am there there is so much to do
I am aimless. I cannot find my rhythm.
The varieties of minutia exceed perception,
But I go there as often as possible
In search of the absolute experience.

There are many deaths,
And little ground.
Thus the graves must be narrow.
About as wide as cots.
But as deep as ever.
Though the ground be frozen
And the digging an agony
The graves
Should not also
Be shallow.
Their narrowness is indignity enough.

§ THE WHITE SHIRTS OF OCEAN AVE. MIAMI BEACH 1992

Everywhere there is the longing of white shirts
For the tenderness of human flesh
To be filling and wrinkling their crispness.

The shaven skulls of coconuts fall to the ground.
The bulldogs walk beside the seawalls on which
Sit the elderly jews in paper noseshades
And senoritas with chins on their drawnup knees
And underthings left home alone.

Darkness enlarges the shrunken.

Under the art-deco pastel neon
The chrome of the parked Harley-Davidsons reflects
The white shirts like mercury on ravens.

These shirts have gleaming eyes.
Underneath them, along the spines, bulge
The wings ready to rip the shirts as they rise
To hover over their longed for, their prey.

But this rarely happens for it is a great commitment
And sacrifice of anonymity.

The shirts rise and fall slowly.
From face to face the eyes seek a sign.
If none comes, por nada, cela viendra.
Another day, another night, our flesh will be human

Our shirts white.

§ FEAR FORCED OUT

Forced into a field of power
As are the pollen filled flowers
About to blow the yellow powder
From themselves,
I shake like a wet dog,
My dazzle increases the sunlight,
I walk out into the sourgrass,
The dandelions about to go brainless,
The golden poppies,
The approaching shower
Of my braincells emptying of fear,
Of their time in the pod, and I
Feel myself forced into a field of power
Like a beetle into clover
Whose wetness once was its horror.

White-coiffed, white-boned, white-eyed,
This is a strange love.
I am the goatman
To your ice nymph,
You sculptress
Of petals
Of salt.
Yet I am drawn toward you
As the red thread is drawn
Through the eye of the needle.
A drop of sweat
Hangs from that needlepoint.
My sweat,
Goat sweat.
And in that droplet
You are reflected
Like a naked woman
In a distant window
All can see,
And see nothing.
What is all this stuff about "the gods"?
What are they to you,
A modern woman?
Did you escape from the Athens National Museum?
Are you a cave-cricket?
Do you have no tan-lines?
Do you eat only crushed ice?
Do you even listen
To the questions
Of *men*?
Are they all liars, betrayers, faithless,
Cruel to the fragile, breakers of hymens,
Piercers of beauty?
Do you really have
Their skins on your wall?
If this is possible in the mind
Could it be modern?
I dont know. I do not.
This is like french-kissing a mummy
Or building a snowman

In a blacksmith's shop.
Hopeless.
I ache like testicles
After five hours of necking
When I read your stark
Poems. Each one a white
Petal veined
With purple, untouchable,
Easily bruised.
And I a proponent
Of the colloquial.
There is no Hell.
There is only separation
And selfish fear, there's only
Difference, that delicious pull
Of the opposite
For its poisonous prey.
I eat you out.
Yes! blasphemous! I do it!
The light and ice
Of you that drip
Down my beard
Taste like rosewater
Of kulfi icecream.
You do not move a muscle.
My erection seems suddenly
Animalian and comic.
I seem an inferior being,
Fixed in time,
Prior to ideas.
Gross, violent, pitiable,
I slobber and grunt, a hog,
While you gaze at space
In pain, in the red
Claws of a thought.
Stiff as coral, runny as brie.
White-coiffed, white-boned, white-eyed,
H.D.

An impossible beauty.
Having come from the sun.
It drips from the interior of the orchid.
It stands watch
In black facemask
Against the pathological.
Its wings are double-layered
And slide closed.
Horror is its fate.
But its duty is good.
To carry the messages.
To make variety the rule.
To confound the authoritarians
Who fear ambiguity
And would have it in its black grave.
Its most compelling power
Is that it is impossible.
Even in a perfect world.
It stands and drips.

§ THE OFFERING

To the somethingness
Which prevents the nothingness
Like Homer's wild boar
From thrashing this way and that
Its white tusks
Through human beings
Like crackling stalks
And to nothing less
I offer this suffering of my father.

If Isaiah was right
And all flesh is grass
I'd like to pass my riding
Mower back and forth across
Your patch of bermuda.
I will work for free.
I will pour my clippings
Under the pecan tree
And take a nap in them.
You will never need
Worry about weeds again.
Dandelions will not
Blemish your putting-green skin
When I begin my gardening.
I will rake you by hand.
Isaiah was a smart man.
He knew the value of pampered trash.
All flesh is grass.

§ *THE PINPOINT OF DEATH*

He gives me the
Ball of
Water to balance.

The dark angels are standing at my window singing
'Miserie, Miserie.'

It is as though a candle the size of a man were
Bending and shaking its duncecap.

Are you going into that pinpoint
And will I be able to go with you?

There is a white donkey
With something silver
In its mouth.
It is eating its rope.

It is drinking the ball of water.

Stream, like darjeeling.
Sunlight in it, amber, wobbling.
Silt barely breathing.
Steelhead fingerlings
Motionless as ornaments in oil.
Each leaf and needle more than mental.
Ask me my name. Who? Water moving
Over moving water. Both halves babble.
My yellow garden-gloves chopped off
And on the railing, drying.
Ferns sleepwalking over the crispness.
Seemingly meaningful deepening of creek.
Real doe breaking the cellophane mythos
And stabbing the gravel with sharp little
Feet. Eyes, two 8-balls. This
Is the afterlife. This here.

§ *THE GOD*

If it is still
And stands in light
Like a leader of objects
And sacrifice being
What choice do we have
But to worship it
With laughter
As one would any
God who has mistaken
His testicles for figs,
And eaten.

§ THE STATUES IN THE ATHENS MUSEUM

Light years beyond bliss
Or despair stand
The white marble statues
In the Athens National Museum.
I think I would like
To make that nymph wet.
I think I would like to kiss my first man.
But they stand
Aloof from the flesh
They are the naked, unblushing, unbleeding
Image of.
Colder to the touch than
A corpse in the coffin.
Prettier, in a fallen way.

§ LOOKING FOR AN APARTMENT IN NEW YORK

Who is the Korean grocer,
    by what light does he sleep, who are
The doves who serve coffee with Arabic accents,
    moving among each other and the steel stools
    like kleenex in airwells, who
Is the condo saleslady in the stilletto heels
    when she is not composed,
Who is the wealthy woman on 5th Ave
    with the ability to speak of the weather
    as though it were holy and the days were numbered,
Who are these people,
And how long will it take me
To sing songs with them in them?

§ REGARDING TORTURE

How silent they were, the Old Masters, about torture.
How lucidly the Greeks argued that slaves
Only told the truth under torture. How
Astounding the ribbed vault of the cathedral,
Like real meat,
And the candles
Dripping blood
Thick as fudge.
How the cruelty goes unmentioned by the Old Masters.
How the individual instances of unspeakable brutality
Were absorbed by time as though time were unable to remember
Its own screamed name.

I was a cowboy
In a former life.
With black boots,
With silver eyes.
My hat was twice
My size. Only
My horror of horses
Kept me from paradise.

§ BECOMING A GODDESS

The woman in the purple dress
Which dares to rhyme with the Miami dusk
(For this is now, and rhyming
Is forbidden, hidden), leaves
The ballroom's deafening jazz
To stand beside the just-rained-on
Stone railing overlooking
The dish-shaped blackgreen fountain
In the patio below her.
Gold floodlights glaze
The carved timbers of the ceiling
Of the room she just left.
Gradually the horizon of Miami
Becomes a darker purple than her dress
And she becomes a goddess of a religion that doesnt exist.

I lost my faith, said the man.
It fell
Into the leaf-skins.
As it lay there
I watched it
Open its hazel animal eyes
And oval mouth
To cry,
"I am nothing,
And now we are equal!"
I jumped up and down for joy
Like a boy who for the first time
Has put his hand into the blouse
Of the Death Goddess.

It is an allegorical beauty
Which raises us
From our jellied state. As when,
In the dream, in the real bed,
Father-in-law enters, so
Recently dead his hair
Is like silver straw, erect,
And his faceskin blotched as if ice
Has burned it, and when I ask,
"Howard, how has it been where you are?"
He mutters,
"Awful, awful," and leaves
By the sliding glass door
With the books he has come for
Under his arm.
It is that beauty raises us
From jelly into. . . . *that* beauty
That redeems us by making us unreal.

§ THE GREEK STATUES

The statue's
Wet
Rock
Dress
Snagged on a thorn
Pulls loose.
                I am naked! This is my story!

We are so white
We must be painted
To find ourselves.

I can tell the blueberry
From the blackberry
And a wolf from a dog
But I cannot pick
My mother
From the other
Women.

A boy
With a girl's lips,
Halfway between godhood
And indifference.

The marble sparkles—

        every penis
        broken off by
        the Christians

—like glass in ice.

The beauty of youth
Melts down the bone.
She is like a candelabra after the guests have gone.

I am an image!
I am not even feces!

§ A PAINTING OF FIRE

Inside its frame
The liquification of flame
Is frozen.
Outside its border
The liquid of order.

§ *DEAR SISTER*

For years I carried
Your strangely archaic poem
In my wallet until
It fell apart.
The vocabulary was icy, exact.
The tension was equal in all elements.
(It was a silk bag with a head in it).
The voice was hushed, bloody. I
Didnt know where in you
That poem came from and never asked.
Now neither of us has it.
And still we go about our
Understated silence with each other.
Playmates to the death.

§ THE SEA AND I

I sit in my folding chair
And the sea comes
Slightly nearer, like an armadillo,
But I stay very still
Because the thing I hate most
Is burning and freezing all at once
Like a torch in a cave movie.
Finally the sun gets fat and orange
And the moon rises
And the sea becomes even more icy and shivery.
I move my chair closer to my house.
People come out
With buckets and flashlights
Looking for crabs. I dont know why they want them.
Crabs are like everything else
Having to do with the sea:
They want to EAT me.
You would think my fear of the sea
Would be sufficient to keep me inland,
But it doesnt because I keep this *secret*.

§ *FOLLOWING RAINSHOWER*

A miracle of mercy is our intelligence
That can perceive the green vine
And purple vineflower canopy
Over the pathway of bricks
Dripping liquid light.
You can paint more than you can see.
You can write
Day and night.

§ *INSOMNIA*

Awake all night.
Sugarcane is purple.
Stars very old, very old.
Look newly minted.
Whip foam, lay eggs, drop dead: cycle of some insects.
'Never be executed on an empty stomach.'
Very old, very old. Dew on dark mint
Slippery as vagina.
Awake all night.
Dead souls
Numerous as light-winkings of water.
Got stopped for no brake-tag
On River Road.
Good thing they werent killers.

§ *LAST FLAMES*

Last flames
Of sunset in water
Are yellow
Like the anger
Of this afternoon.

A dry silver before nightfall
Seems to soothe
The waves.
They become tiny and silver until like a mirror.

Im not angry anymore.
The sea is black, the sky is black, there's no horizon.
Im afraid to be angry.

§ LIKE A MAN IN A TOPHAT IN AN OLD BOOK UNDER A STREETLAMP LIGHTING HIS PIPE YOU LIVE FOREVER

Snow falls on the ocean.
The whitespace masturbates with a candle.
I think of you.
Let it snow.
Let the mindpearl dissolve in the object.
We imagine the moments in spotlight:
As they were
When we were.
A cake. A pearl. A snarling dog.
The sea, for the first time, *liquid*.
And we thought a skeleton was driving.

She found it difficult to be faithful
To a traveling salesman from Waco
Since she spent her whole so-called life
In a double-wide trailer by the Texaco station
In cut-off jeans and a white spandex halter,
Waiting. So one day this guy getting gas saw her
On the steps of the trailer shaking a dustmop
And came over. "You married?" he asked.
"A little," she answered,
And let her head flop slightly, coquetishly, sideways.
"Well then," he said, "can I visit?"
"Well, hell, I guess," and the screendoor went
Whack!
In about half an hour he came out.
She stood on the gravel in her robe
As he drove off toward Midland-Odessa,
Put her hands on her hips like a teacher
And said to herself, Well, fuck you, too,
And went back into her trailer.

§ A GREAT KAZOO FOR ONE KILLED BY A SNIPER

Roll out the sheet of aluminum foil
For him hit by the sniper.
For he has bought the creamy froth
Of the moment, he
Has scraped the cherry.
Prepare for him the big
Kazoo, with partridges, with green wine, with bamboo
Full of chestnuts.
For he has ignited
The cane. Out of a tree
Out of a tree
Came the flash he experienced
As impact, thinking, "Oh!
Now I go to the great kazoo!
Make my bed light
So the living wont drop me!"
So we roll out the eight feet
Of aluminum foil.
And we wrap him thus
Like the great potato we knew, and
We dip him in the boiling green wine,
And what of him we dont eat we drink, singing,
"O, you, who got sapped, who sucked up the froth, who
Scraped the cherry, who felt the thud, who fills our bellies,
Who died a warrior, this great kazoo is for you!"

At this time
Winter begins
To yield to Spring.
Already something
Resembling
Tumescence
In the branches
Attracts our
Attention. Other
Tensions also
Seem to stiffen
The garden. They
Are as yet
Undefinable but
Clearly it is
Too late to
Withdraw the green
Ejaculate.

With each egg she lays
The turtle sheds a milky tear.
No one knows why.

"I lost control.
My milk wouldnt come down.
My baby turned red in the cradle.
Crying & crying & crying.
I pressed a pillow against her face.
When she stopped moving
I called them and said Come get me."

The zodiac is hemmorhaging.

Puffed up, ready for entry, snake,
Its head flat and wide, like a sandal,
Shovels forward, a kind of evil shuffle
Sideways, up and down.

In heaven
The roach
Is a jewel.

The typos of the giant is that he is stupid,
The typos of the dwarf
That he is clever and impotent, of the princess
That she lowers her chin and coos.

Wont you come home Johnny, wont you?

She wept, she
Slept with Sam, whose glamor
Was in power, who drank
With either hand.

The whole crystal is in itself.

Junk dream wastes veal.
Plump crow tastes evil.
Thieves' yield gelds will.

Now I am free.

All day, ugh, I am drugged
By the drug supposed to make me happy.
I doze as I read. Everything seems unfriendly.
A sudden rainshower, flashpan of lightning,
Thunder gloomily ripening,
Then the sunshine again, and dew gems
All over the deck. I am so sleepy.
I wish happiness would come soon
Or else I might fall asleep
And miss the boat to Heaven,
And that would be a big waste given
The time Ive invested in transcending the trivial,
Especially in an age when transcendence
Is dismissed as intellectual snobbery.
I still say someday I will be able
To walk into a painting just like into a barbershop
And say, I am here, Yes, I am from the real world,
And the barbers will crowd around me
And joyously clack their scissors.
If only I could shake this drowsiness
Brought on by the drug intended to bring me happiness,
And get down to painting, and wake
Into the rainshower that makes
Everything shiver with fate.

§ TEA TIME

I must think this through: is
Drinking tea with him
At the outside table
As the fog crests
Better than excess?
Every gesture of his implies
That the lightning-bug is precisely
As crazy as something should get.
More than that is just Germans
In bloody aprons drinking
Beer under the gutless moon.
From teaspout, the spirit, the parable, the example.
So I said to him,
"I thought I had broken the mirror between the book
And the world."
And he said, his teacup trembling, his wife newly dead,
"You were young."

§ *THE PAGES*

The skeleton
In the etching
Delicately
Picks
The ink apple.

Turn the page.

A ball of snow
Cannot be sold
Into slavery.

Shakespeare was obsessed
With juicy youth.
The buttery boys of Italian
Statues and creamy marble Greeks
Should be proof enough. In rotting
Venice Thomas Mann imagined Tonio
As unsexed flesh before Death
Knows it's there.
It's no new thing for one
To see oneself removed from
Life like a rotted tooth
While just across the street
A slender hairless nymph consumes
A banana split with complete indifference.

§ PITY

In pitiless sun
The farmer is
Beating his donkey.

Only its brown eyes
Drifting in pain
From side to side

Move.

The chandeliers
In the antique stores
Drip blood
Because without slavery
They would never have been.
And yet they remind the spirit of itself.

"No thank you," we say,
As when refusing
Cream with our coffee,
But the ghost insists,
Pushes open the back porch screen
And sits down in the kitchen:
Father, it says, I-have-been-thinking-of-you.

My prowling, growling swan,
Well aware that my soul
Is nourished by roses
Disguised as live coals,
Rustles from her crowded clothes,
For she as naked image knows
How to make the living stiffen
And the corpses stretch and yawn:
My darling prowling growling swan.

If he says
The river bends
The river bends.
He says there is
A hangman in the ground
A hangman stands
Where he says.
          For he is Leadbelly.

Her voice
Is as close to insanity
As the white moth
On the grey wall
Is to its shadow.

The present
Is mostly sweet.
History is mostly
Feet in large jars.

He witheld affection
So that his attentions
To whomever he eventually gave them
Were an H-bomb of long-stemmed roses.

My love and I are in accord
That we are less cowardly than the stars.

Starlight in the fishpond.
The slugs wetly advanced.
Water condensed on the grassblades.
Boneless vines, here she comes.
The crystalization, I could hear it.
Out of my skin slid my mind.
Nearby what she leaked
I licked. Like the fishpond
Filled with black water and stars
She filled me.
The slugs made bulletholes in the mushrooms.
The greenhouse windows
Seethed with vulvas. Crackling and suction.
But I stuck like the male vine.
On my hands she melted.
She was shellac and fishscales.
We, winking valves.
The slugs retreated over the orderly dirt.
We crept, stuck.
One of the violent harmonies.

The crape myrtles are nearly naked.
Only faint pink hairs.
Still the hibiscuses widen their naive masks.
The cold has not been sufficient
To turn the banana leaves to slime.
Chameleon lizards cannot decide whether to choose
The heat of the steel or the cool of the steel's shadow.

§ *THE CATALOG GODDESSES*

I stare down at the gossamer
Flounce of blond tigress
With the pelvis of perfume
In the Bloomingdale's Catalog.
Aching that she not snub me
As the bumpkin I am, aching
For the six-foot kitten with eyes
So blue they show through her sunglasses.
In the catalog, flat and cool,
In her own rectangle, by which is written, "Rejoice
At the return of the boy coat
In camel." They can do no wrong,
These carnal crushed-sequined halter-sheathed
Keyholed snapbottom lycra
Felines in fuchsia and silver.
I keep the catalog beside the toilet.
I open it and feel like one of their
Buttery-soft black leather purses and
Make sounds like a tray of ice cubes
Thrust under running hot water.

§ TOUCHING

The weeping willows
Touch us all over. It
Is impossible to move
Untouched among them.
Their touching is a way to make certain
We continue to care for
What they have despaired of.

§ THE TAPEWORM

Can you find the tapeworm
In the human heart
Without visiting Hell?

In what do you believe?
Leafless as hairs, the winter trees.
The burning chill
As face passes face, eyes
Vivid as tropical fish
In the fluorescence of the winter streets.
Do you believe in these?

Time to breed. Time
To quicken.
Agreed.

The green limes
Will bend the branches, sicken
Us with their promise.
But we must feed on

Them or the tapeworm
Will peer from
Our anuses
And crawl up our backs

And squeeze our brains
From our ears and nostrils.
So it is into the orchard
Planted on the burial

Site
We must go to copulate.
Until we are as satiated
As sleeping children.

The icy distance
Of millions
Of lights
Of windows
They are not molecules
Without biographies
They are the eyes
Wet with brain
They are the sparkle on black water.

Come near
The soft hole
Of the voice.

It is aching
And
Wants.

Until you do
The white rose
Of your red life

Will nourish the worm.

Hell opens. The ghosts,
The fears, enter,
Dragged by the hair
Into the glimmer of eyes and mouths.
There the soul is naked.
It sobs in the mirror

That shivers like windblown water.
It hears its name cried
And obeys the cry and enters.
Says the Shade: "I am
Your catfur. Stroke me
And be guided. For the path here
Is slippery
And if you fall
You fall forever. Heed
My sparkle. Step only in
My hoofprints.
Follow."

Only the tapeworm's image
Can lure the tapeworm
From its lair.

It will try to enter
The reflection
Of its own intestines.

I was afraid,
But that was no new thing.
What was new was
The intimacy of the distance.
The nakedness of the trees.
The water's black clarity.
The eyes of the strangers,
Like living brain.
The differences between things.

Pentheus, the proud boy
Humiliated and slaughtered by Dionysus
In Euripides' play *The Bacchae*,
I knew in the Haight-Ashbury
When his name was Stan Rice.
He lived in what is now the Free Clinic
On Clayton Street and kept
By his typewriter always a 2 lb. coffee can
Of seedless and stemless pot, packed
Smooth as sand. And nothing
Could hurt him. Nothing. Threw
Spaghetti on the ceiling and it stuck,
Spelling his war-name. Bore down
On fake gods, Dionysus' Diggers, anti-art
Hippies, chicks prey to black rapists,
Returned to Nature, swam naked, found in communes
Fascism and women as role-slaves.
On those he bore down, aloof,
Writing his raw poems, this
Pentheus, never a hippy, but stayed
Stoned, as a personal power.
And left the Haight-Ashbury
After the police cracked down.
Blue apes, truly. Virtual
Civil war in the streets. S. Rice
Emerged as Pentheus in Berkeley.
Bore down on Leftists,
And saw with his own
Drunk slit eyes the Bacchae
Go bad, the Black Panthers rise,
Thugs with just enough Marx
To focus their thuggery, and Pentheus
Scorned them too, and the white Maoists
Intolerant as Inquisitors, and eventually
The feminists with their dogmas and
Straight thornless path to censorship.
I knew him still as invincible, cutting
His poems from skin, spy and beholder
In the midst of the faux-revolutionaries
In leafy Berkeley, invisible there. And then

The god came to punish his arrogance.
Cut off his child's head, held it up
And cried Look! S. R. Pentheus!
You mocked necessity, you put your
Youthful power against our
God's griefless strength. Now look at
Your legacy on this stick. Can your coffee can
Packed smooth with pot
Make this vanish? Are you still
Invulnerable? And Stan
Rice stiffened, melted, stiffened, saw
Pentheus flicker, age,
Straight out of Peoples Park,
Down the hallways of Kaiser Hospital,
Pulled by a bull to Hell.

A NOTE ABOUT THE AUTHOR

Stan Rice was associated for many years with San Francisco
State University, as assistant director of the Poetry Center,
and then as chairman of the Creative Writing Department.
He is the author of four earlier books of poems. He
received the Academy of American Poets Edgar Allan Poe
Award for the third of these, to acknowledge the
continuing achievement of a poet under forty-five. He now
lives in New Orleans.

A NOTE ON THE TYPE

The text of this book was set in Sabon, a type face
designed by Jan Tschichold (1902–1974), the well-known
German typographer. Because it was designed in Frankfurt,
Sabon was named for the famous Frankfurt type founder
Jacques Sabon, who died in 1850 while manager of the
Egenolff foundry.

Based loosely on the original designs of Claude Garamond
(c. 1480–1561), Sabon is unique in that it was explicitly
designed for hot-metal composition on both the Monotype
and Linotype machines as well as for film composition.

Composition by Creative Graphics Inc.
Allentown, Pennsylvania
Printed and bound by Quebecor Printing
Kingsport, Tennessee
Designed by Harry Ford